Joy to the World!

CAROLS SELECTED BY MAUREEN FORRESTER

ILLUSTRATED BY Frances Tyrrell

Dutton Children's Books   New York

*To my grandchildren, Laura, Thomas, David,
Ryan, Galen, Hayley, Henry, and Hannah*
M.F.

*To the children at the
Scott Mission Daycare Centre*
F.T.

The Publisher gratefully acknowledges the kind help of Charles Heller
in providing the musical arrangements.

The Publisher also wishes to acknowledge the contribution of Avril Tyrrell
in creating the concept for this book.

Library of Congress Cataloging-in-Publication Data

Joy to the world!/Christmas carols selected by Maureen Forrester;
illustrated by Frances Tyrrell.—1st American ed.
1 score.
For voice and piano, with interlinear words.
ISBN 0-525-45169-2
1. Christmas music—Juvenile.   2. Carols, English—Juvenile.
I. Forrester, Maureen.   II. Tyrrell, Frances, ill.
M2191.C5J8   1993   93-2894   CIP   AC M

First published in the United States 1993 by Dutton Children's Books,
a division of Penguin Books USA Inc.
375 Hudson Street, New York, New York 10014

Originally published in Canada 1992 by Lester Publishing Limited, Toronto
Display Typography by Amy Berniker
Printed and bound in Canada
First American Edition
1 3 5 7 9 10 8 6 4 2

Contents

Introduction

"Make a joyful noise unto the Lord, all the earth . . ." — PSALM 98

The carols in this book have been passed down to us from many sources. "The Friendly Beasts" originated in a medieval passion play that was first performed eight hundred years ago in France. "Go Tell It on the Mountain" is a spiritual with roots deep in Africa. "Foom, Foom, Foom!" is a merry dancing tune from Catalonia. "Silent Night" was written in an Austrian village by a young priest and the local schoolmaster to make up for the disappointment of a broken church organ at Christmas time. A lovely legend describes how angels visited a monk named Henry Suso while he slept and left him with an extraordinary gift — the hymn "In Dulci Jubilo."

Through long centuries, people all over the world — in chilly village churches, in grand cathedrals, on frosty street corners, and in their own cosy sitting-rooms — have gathered to sing carols at Christmas time: music that reaffirms our longing for joy and peace.

The carols, old and new, that have been selected for *Joy to the World!* are set in our own time and place because we take part in a time-honored and glorious tradition when we make this music our own.

Deck the Halls

Traditional Welsh

Traditional Welsh

Arranged by C.H.

1. Deck the halls with boughs of hol - ly, Fa la la la la la la la la;

'Tis the sea - son to be jol - ly, Fa la la la la la la la la.

Don we now our gay ap - par - el, Fa la la la la la la la la.

Troll the an - cient Christ - mas car - ol, Fa la la la la la la la la!

2.

See the blazing yule before us,
Fa-la-la-la-la, la-la-la-la;
Strike the harp and join the chorus,
Fa-la-la-la-la, la-la-la-la.
Follow me in merry measure,
Fa-la-la, la-la-la, la-la-la.
While I sing of Yuletide treasure,
Fa-la-la-la-la, la-la-la-la.

3.

Fast away the old year passes,
Fa-la-la-la-la, la-la-la-la;
Hail the new, ye lads and lasses,
Fa-la-la-la-la, la-la-la-la.
Sing we joyous all together,
Fa-la-la, la-la-la, la-la-la.
Heedless of the wind and weather,
Fa-la-la-la-la, la-la-la-la!

The Friendly Beasts

Robert Davis

Medieval French

Arranged by C.H.

Allegretto (like bagpipes)

1. Je - sus, our bro - ther, kind and good, Was hum - bly born in a sta - ble

* grace notes in the right hand may be played ad lib.

rude, And the friend - ly beasts a - round Him stood; Je - sus, our bro - ther, kind and good.

Alternative accompaniment for last verse

slower

5. Thus ev - 'ry beast by some good spell, In the sta - ble dark was glad to tell of the

f

allarg. _ _ _

gift he gave Em - man - u - el, the gift he gave Em - man - u - el. _____

2.
"I," said the donkey, shaggy and brown,
"I carried His mother up hill and down;
I carried her safely to Bethlehem town.
I," said the donkey, shaggy and brown.

3.
"I," said the sheep with curly horn,
"I gave Him my wool for His blanket warm,
He wore my coat on Christmas morn.
I," said the sheep with curly horn.

4.
"I," said the camel, yellow and black,
"Over the desert, upon my back,
I brought Him a gift in the Wise Men's pack.
I," said the camel, yellow and black.

The First Nowell

Traditional

Traditional

Arranged by C.H.

f

1. The _ first _ Now - ell the _ an - gel did say Was to cer - tain poor shep - herds in fields as they lay; In _ fields _ where _ they lay _ keep - ing their sheep, On a cold win - ter's night _ that was _ so deep. Now - ell, _ Now - ell, Now - ell, Now - ell, Born is the King _ of Is - ra - el.

2.	3.	4.
They looked up and saw a star	And by the light of that same star	This star drew nigh to the northwest,
Shining in the east, beyond them far,	Three wise men came from country far;	O'er Bethlehem it took its rest;
And to the earth it gave great light,	To seek for a King was their intent,	And there it did stop and stay,
And so it continued both day and night.	And to follow the star wherever it went.	Right over the place where Jesus lay.
Refrain:	*Refrain:*	*Refrain:*
Nowell, Nowell, Nowell, Nowell.		
Born is the King of Israel.		

10

Foom, Foom, Foom!

Traditional Catalonian

Traditional Catalonian

Arranged by C.H.

2.
Little birds fly from the woods,
    sing foom, foom, foom!
Little birds fly from the woods,
    sing foom, foom, foom!
Leave the little ones at home,
Abandon them, abandon them;
From a cozy nest to please us
For the little baby Jesus,
Foom, foom, foom!

3.
Little stars light up the sky,
    sing foom, foom, foom!
Little stars light up the sky,
    sing foom, foom, foom!
You may look at Jesus crying
But yourselves must not be crying;
Make the dark night glitter lightly,
Make it twinkle purely, brightly,
Foom, foom, foom!

Silent Night

Joseph Mohr (1792-1848)

Franz Xavier Gruber (1787-1863)

Arranged by C.H.

2.

Silent night, holy night!
Shepherds quake at the sight,
Glories stream from heaven afar,
Heavenly hosts sing alleluia;
Christ the Savior is born!
Christ the Savior is born!

3.

Silent night, holy night!
Wondrous star, lend thy light!
With the angels let us sing
Alleluia to our King!
Christ the Savior is here,
Christ the Savior is here!

Joy to the World!

Isaac Watts (1674-1748)

Unknown

Arranged by C.H.

ev - 'ry__ heart____ pre - pare__ Him__ room,____ and heav'n and na - ture_ sing, And_

heav'n and na - ture_ sing, And_ heav'n,____ and heav'n____ and na - ture sing.

2.

Joy to the world! the Savior reigns;

Let men their songs employ;

While fields and floods, rocks, hills and plains,

Repeat the sounding joy,

Repeat the sounding joy,

Repeat, repeat the sounding joy.

3.

He rules the earth with truth and grace,

And makes the nations prove

The glories of His righteousness,

And wonders of His love,

And wonders of His love,

And wonders, wonders of His love.

16

In Dulci Jubilo

Henry Suso (fl. 14th century)

Henry Suso

Arranged by C.H.

1. In dul-ci ju-bi-lo _____ Let us our hom-age show; _____ Our heart's joy re-clin-eth _____ In prae-se-pi-o _____ And like a bright star shin-eth Ma-tris in gre-mi-o; _____ Al-pha es et O, _____ Al-pha es et O.

(rit. last time)

2.

O *patris caritas*
O *nati lenitas,*
Deeply were we stained
Per nostra crimina
But Thou hast for us gained
Coelorum gaudia.
O that we were there,
O that we were there.

3.

Ubi sunt gaudia
If that they be not there?
There are angels singing
Nova cantica,
There the bells are ringing
In regis curia.
O that we were there!
O that we were there!

Go Tell It on the Mountain

American Spiritual

American Spiritual

Arranged by C.H.

2.
He made me watchman
    up on the city wall,
And if I am a Christian,
    I am the least of all.
Oh! Go tell it on the mountain,
    over the hills and everywhere,
Go tell it on the mountain
    that Jesus Christ is born!

Patapan

Bernard de la Monnoye (1641-1728)

Burgundian, 17th century

Arranged by C.H.

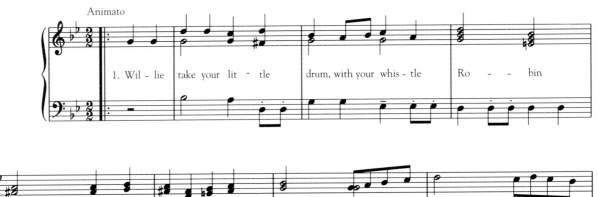

1. Wil - lie take your lit - tle drum, with your whis - tle Ro - bin come! When we hear the fife and drum, Tu - re - lu - re - lu, pa - ta - pa - ta - pan, When we hear the fife and drum, Christ - mas should be frol - ic - some!

2.	3.
Thus the men of olden days	God and man are now become
Loved the King of kings to praise:	More at one than fife and drum.
When they hear the fife and drum,	When you hear the fife and drum,
Turelurelu, patapatapan,	*Turelurelu, patapatapan,*
When they hear the fife and drum,	When you hear the fife and drum,
Sure our children won't be dumb!	Dance, and make the village hum!

Angels We Have Heard on High

Traditional French

Traditional French

Arranged by C.H.

Moderato

1. An - gels we have heard on high, sweet - ly sing - ing o'er the plains,

And the __ moun - tains __ in re - ply, Ech - o - ing their __ joy - ous strains.

Glo - - - - - ri - a in ex - cel - sis De - o,

Glo - - - - - ri - a in ex - cel - sis De - o.

(Ped. ad lib.)

2.

Shepherds, why this jubilee?

Why your joyous strains prolong?

What the gladsome tidings be,

Which inspire your heavenly song?

Gloria in excelsis Deo,

Gloria in excelsis Deo.

3.

Come to Bethlehem and see

Him whose birth the angels sing;

Come, adore on bended knee,

Christ the Lord, the newborn King.

Gloria in excelsis Deo,

Gloria in excelsis Deo.

I Saw Three Ships

Traditional

Traditional

Arranged by C.H.

3.

Our Savior, Jesus Christ, was there,

On Christmas Day, on Christmas Day;

Our Savior, Jesus Christ, was there,

On Christmas Day in the morning.

4.

Pray, whither sailed those ships all three?

5.

O, they sailed into Bethlehem.

6.

And all the bells on earth shall ring.

7.

Then let us all rejoice again!

Rocking

Traditional Czech

Translated by "O.B.C"

Traditional Czech

Arranged by C.H.

Andante

p

Ped. ad lib

1. Lit - tle Je - sus sweet - ly ___ sleep,

do not ___ stir; We will ___ lend a ___ coat of ___ fur, We will rock you

rock you, rock you, We will rock you, rock you, rock you: See the fur to

keep you ___ warm, Snug - ly ___ round your ___ ti - ny ___ form.

(last time) D.C.

(last time)

2.

Mary's little Baby, sleep, sweetly sleep,

Sleep in comfort, slumber deep;

We will rock you, rock you, rock you,

We will rock you, rock you, rock you:

We will serve you all we can,

Darling, darling little man.

Notes on the Carols

DECK THE HALLS

Many of our best-loved Christmas carols have come to us through a combination of two distinct types of music: the secular and the religious. The popular Welsh carol "Deck the Halls" contains no religious sentiments, but it is a fine way to celebrate the joy of the season. Although we do not know who wrote it or when it was written, the melody was so well known by the eighteenth century that Mozart used it in a duet for violin and piano.

THE FRIENDLY BEASTS

For years people believed that this was a twelfth-century English carol, but research has established its ancient French roots. It originated as part of a medieval mystery play, the *Fête de l'âne* (The Donkey's Festival), which was performed each Christmas in Beauvais, France, as a celebration of the Israelites' flight from Egypt. An English writer of hymns, Richard Redhead, revived the melody in the 1850s. Robert Davis wrote the words in New York City in the early 1900s.

THE FIRST NOWELL

It is strange that although this carol is so popular we know very little about its author or its source. Scholars believe that it may have originated in France many centuries ago, but the first printed version we have found comes from William Sandys in his important 1833 collection of Christmas music.

FOOM, FOOM, FOOM!

Catalonia is a distinct part of Spain with its own language and its own proud traditions. This lovely, rollicking carol, which reminds us that people originally danced to many sacred songs, is still popular throughout Spain today.

SILENT NIGHT

The organ was out of order in the little Church of St. Nikola in Oberndorf, Austria, and Christmas was fast approaching. The twenty-six-year-old pastor, Joseph Mohr, wanted to make up for the congregation's disappointment by composing a special hymn for the season. He gave the lyrics to his friend Franz Gruber, the village schoolteacher and church organist. Within the day, Gruber had composed the music. Mohr and Gruber's carol, "Silent Night," was heard for the first time on Christmas Eve, 1818, and soon became very popular.

JOY TO THE WORLD!

The melody is often incorrectly attributed to George Frideric Handel, but the fact is that we do not know who is responsible for this glorious music. The words were written by Isaac Watts, who published the verses in 1719 as part of the *Psalms of David, Imitated in the Language of the New Testament*. From the 98th Psalm:

> "Make a joyful noise unto the Lord, all the earth; make a loud noise, and rejoice and sing praise!"

IN DULCI JUBILO

We know that this splendid carol was sung at the Moravian Mission in what is now Bethlehem, Pennsylvania, on September 14, 1745, in thirteen languages, including Wendish, Mohawk, Latin, Greek, and German. But there is a far older legend surrounding its origins. Henry Suso, a Dominican mystic who lived in the fourteenth century, is said to have dreamed of a ring of dancing angels who presented him with the carol as he slept.

GO TELL IT ON THE MOUNTAIN

"Go Tell It on the Mountain" is probably the most famous Christmas carol to come from the great tradition of gospel music in the United States. The slaves who toiled in the southern states developed a glorious body of music that drew heavily on the rhythms and call-and-response patterns of their African heritage. As with most spirituals, we do not know the author or the composer.

PATAPAN

Many historians believe that carols have grown out of a combination of ancient religious hymns and dance music. The marching tempo of "Patapan" seems to invite dancers to step in time with the music. Bernard de la Monnoye (1641-1728) is credited with setting words to this cheery Burgundian melody. In 1842, "Patapan" appeared for the first time in written form in a collection entitled *Noëls bourguignons de la Monnoye*.

ANGELS WE HAVE HEARD ON HIGH

Although some people believe that this hymn originated in the second century, it is more likely that it is less than three hundred years old. Historians have traced it both to France and to Quebec.

I SAW THREE SHIPS

This anonymous carol has been sung in Great Britain for at least five hundred years and perhaps more. It appeared in the great collection by William Sandys that was published in 1833. The image of three ships sailing, bearing the Magi and their gifts for the Holy Family or, in the very early versions, bearing the Holy Family itself, was a popular one.

ROCKING

The Oxford Book of Carols (1925) is the source for the translation of this sweet Christmas lullaby. We know that it is of Czech origin, but the author and composer are both anonymous.

ILLUSTRATOR'S NOTES

All the paintings were originally done in watercolor on Arches satin finish 100% rag paper.

The illustrator wishes to thank all the people who helped make these illustrations possible. They include:

The children and staff of the Scott Mission Daycare Centre, Toronto, with special thanks to Bill Whitehouse; the teachers, musicians, and children of the First Baptist Church, Toronto; the Grace Anglican Church Memorial Handbell Choir, Milton, Ontario; the Sisters of St. Joseph's of Hamilton, Ontario; Lauren Breckon of Oakville, Ontario; Evan Davies and Jacob Ross of London, Ontario; Doug and Yvonne Tyrrell of Etobicoke, Ontario; and all the people who skate on the creek, create magical windows, make lovely music, help each other, and were the inspiration for this book. A special thank you to Avril Tyrrell for conceiving and initiating this project. The paintings for "Angels We Have Heard on High" and "In Dulci Jubilo" are from the private collections of Hedi Nowak, Harrop House, Milton, Ontario, and Janet Baker of Mississauga, Ontario.